THIS BOOK BELONGS TO

Art
DESIGN

We have put a lot of effort to prevent any bleeding through the pages however bleeding still may occur when using water-based supplies such as watercolor markers and more here's a tip you can slip a piece of board behind the white paper to avoid casting hue to the next page enjoy.

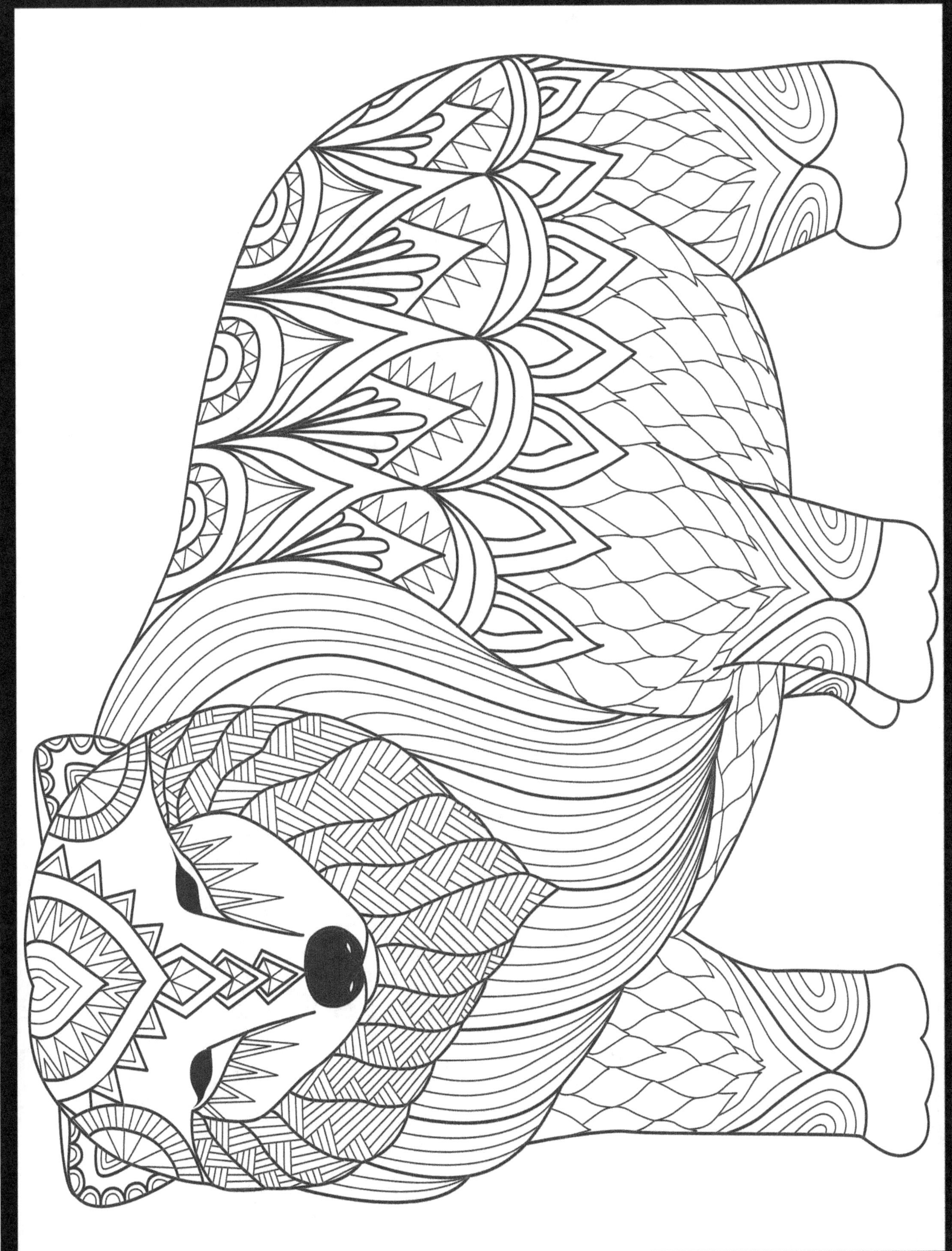

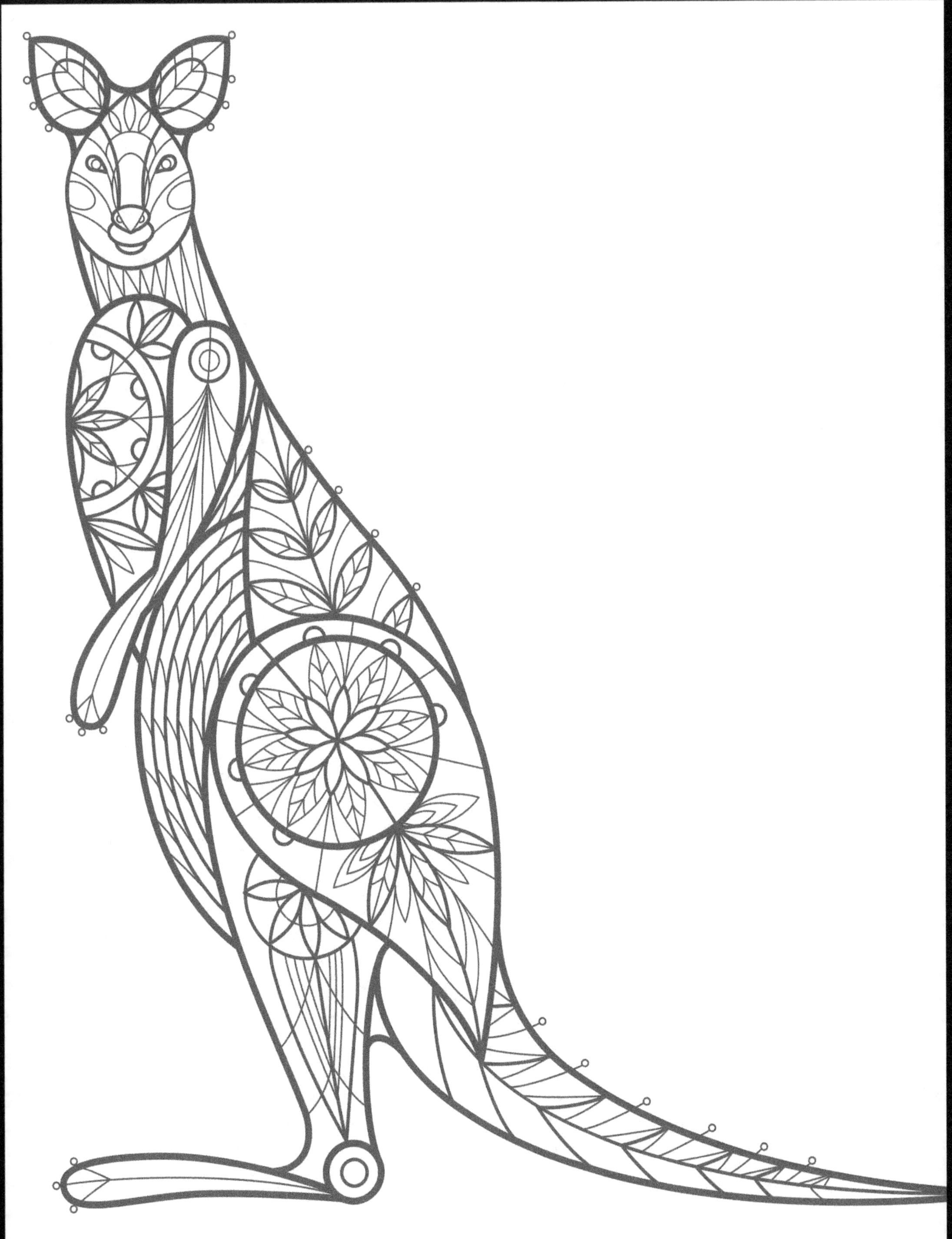

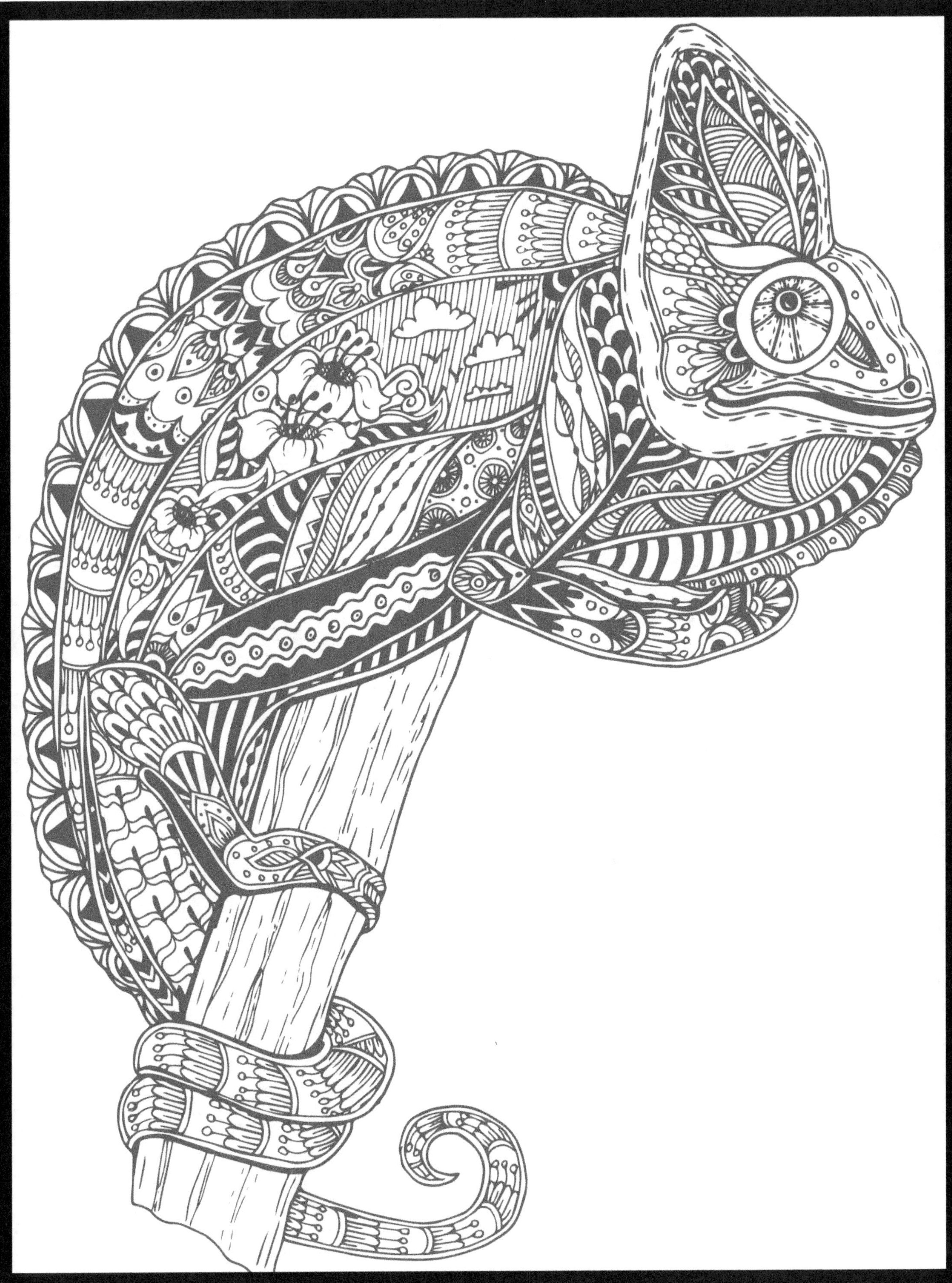

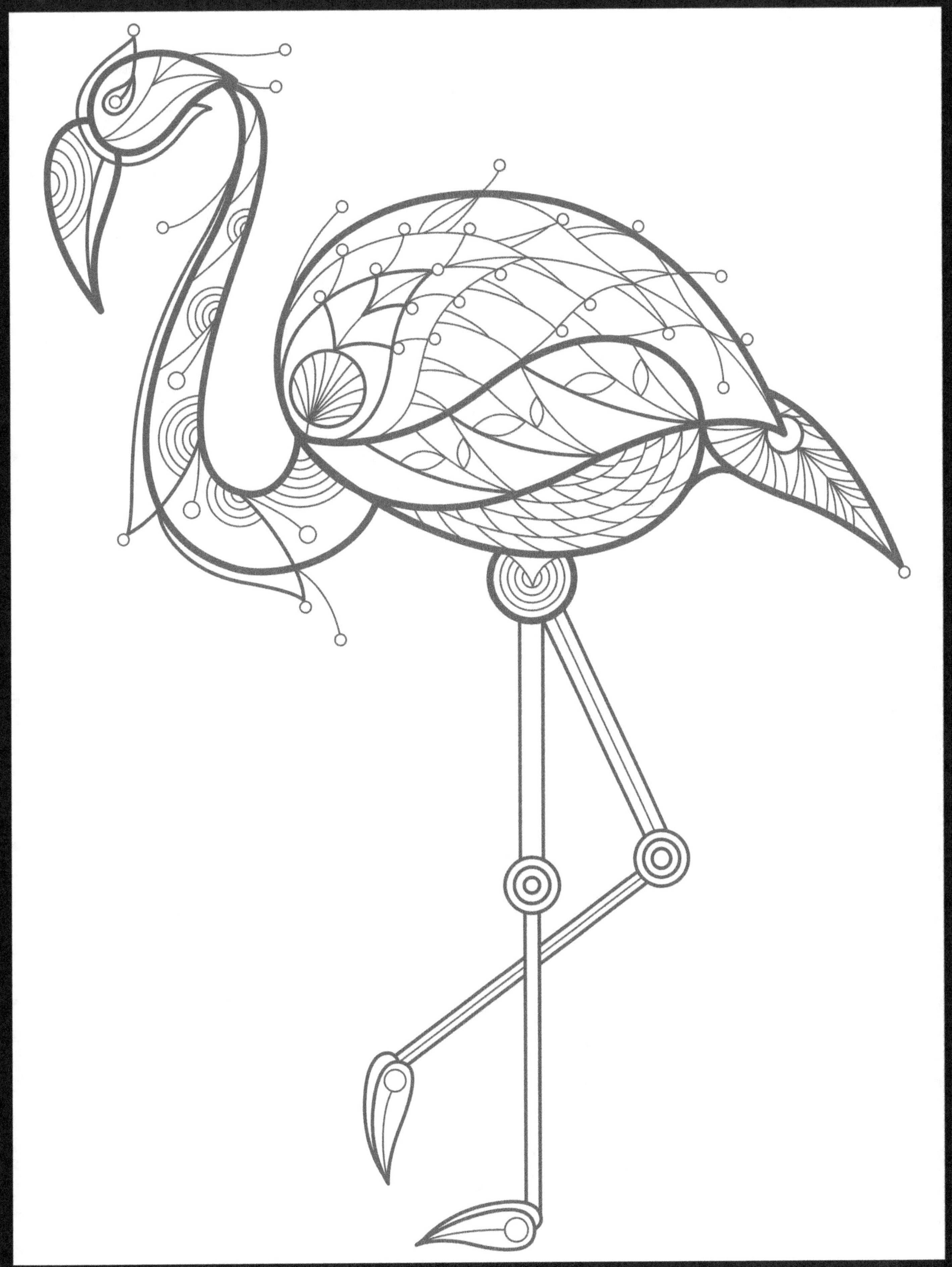

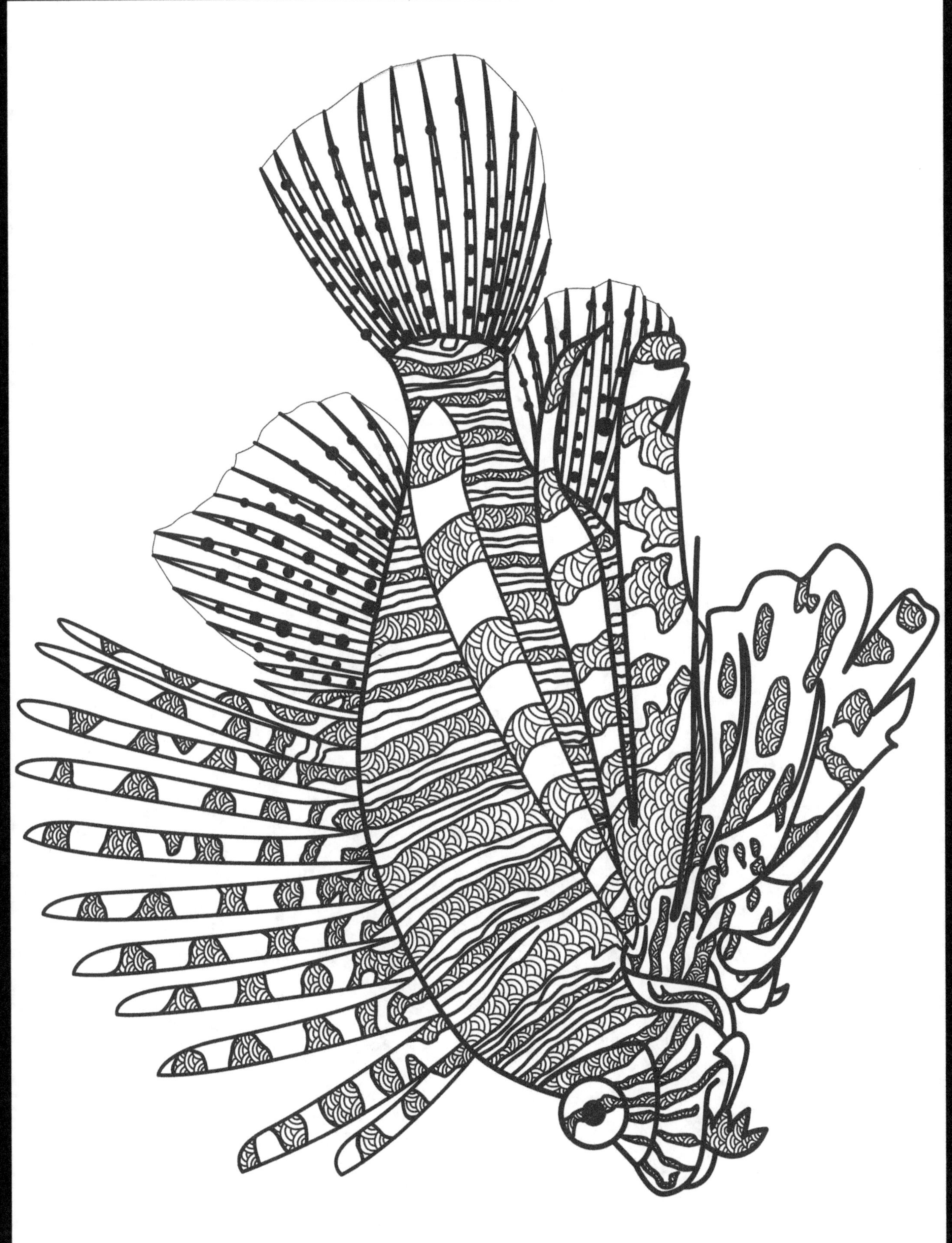

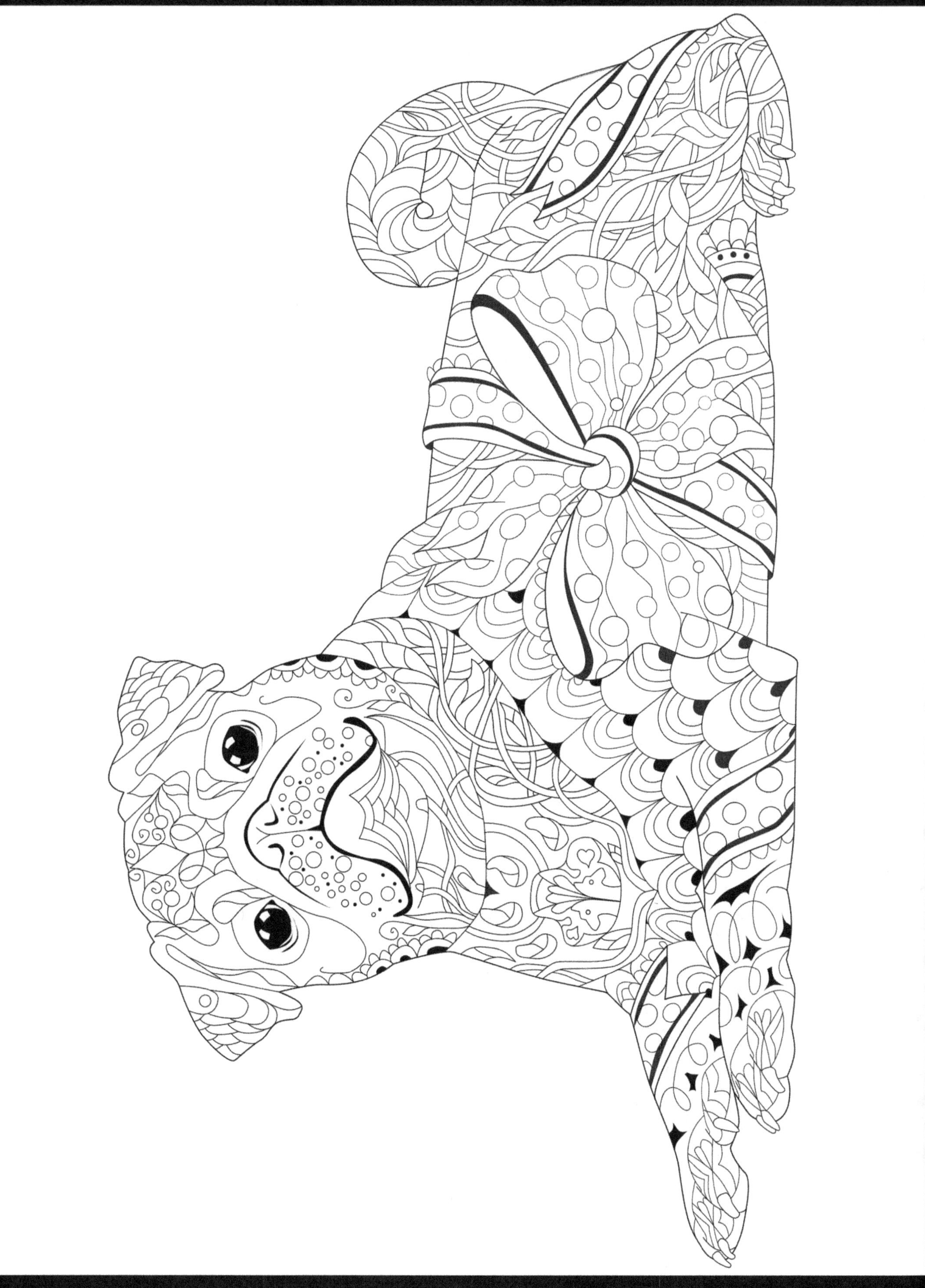

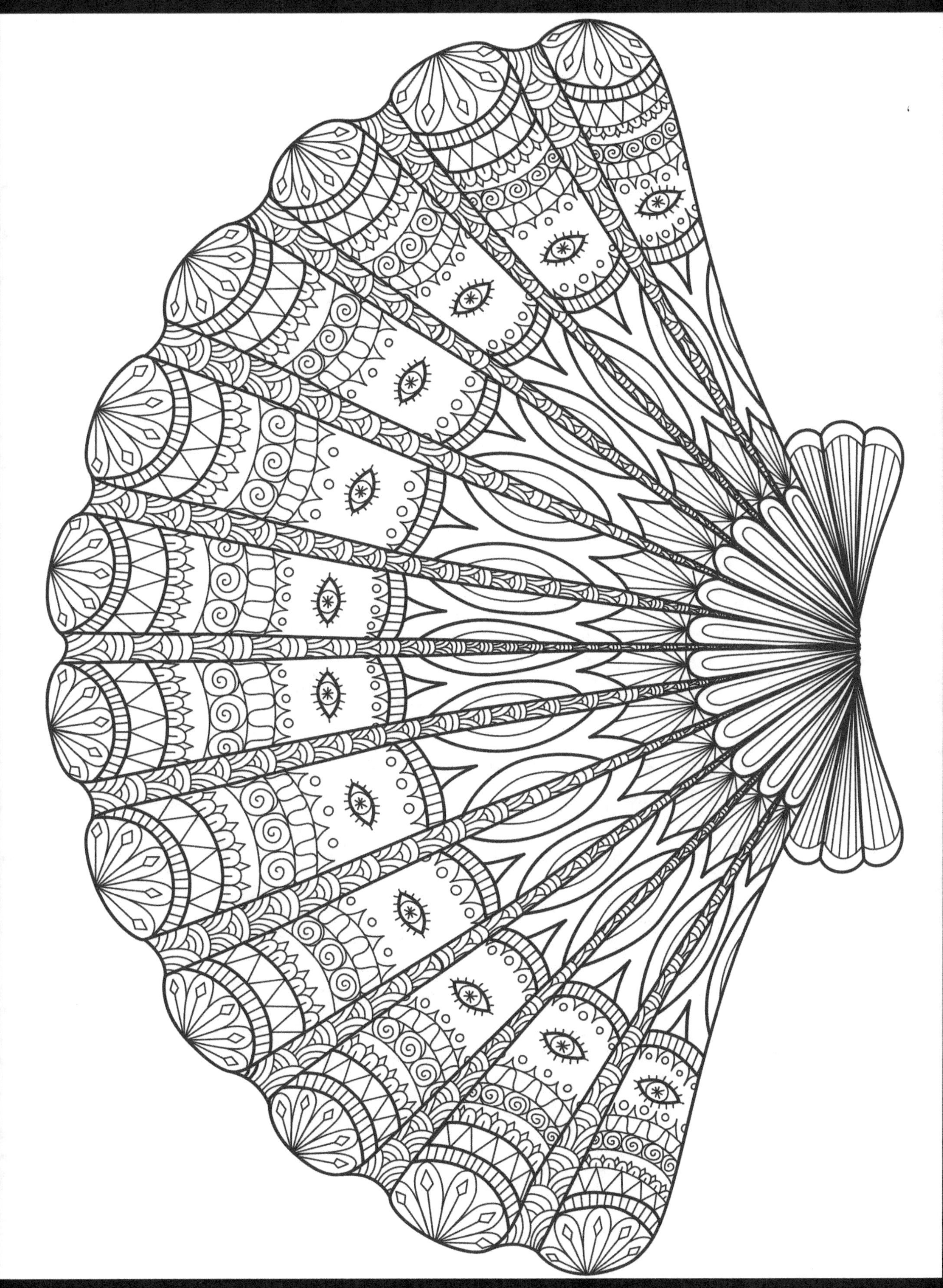

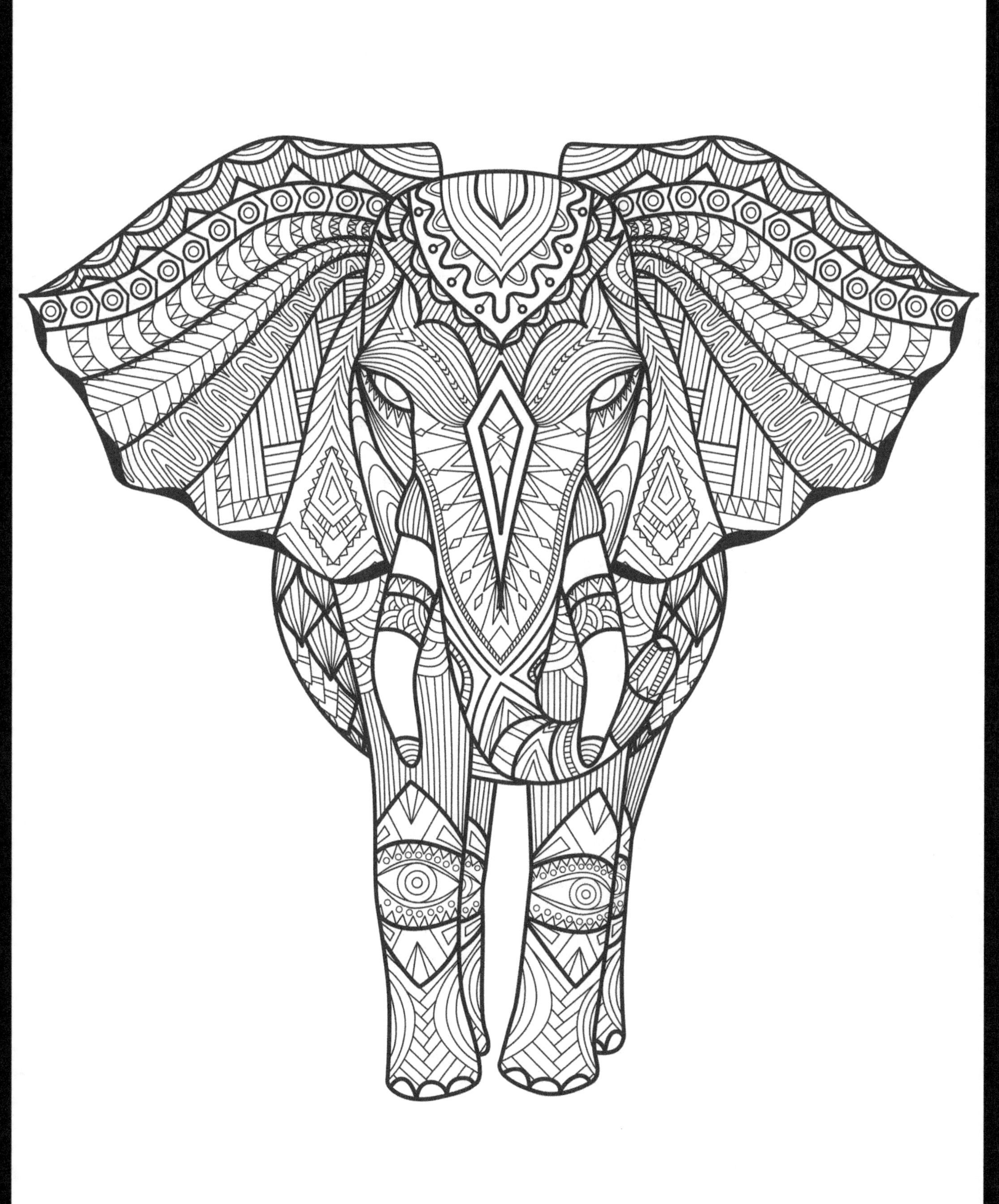

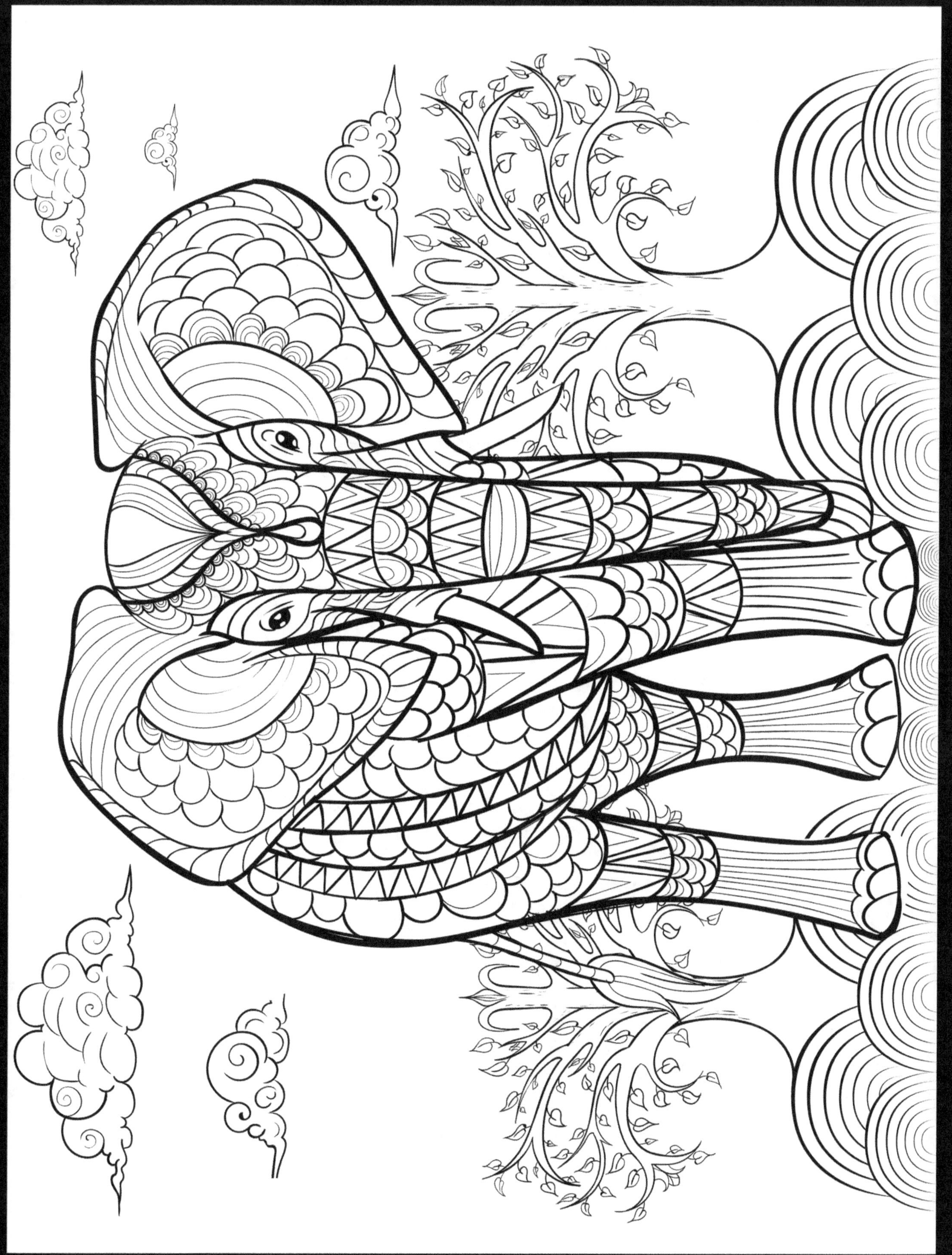

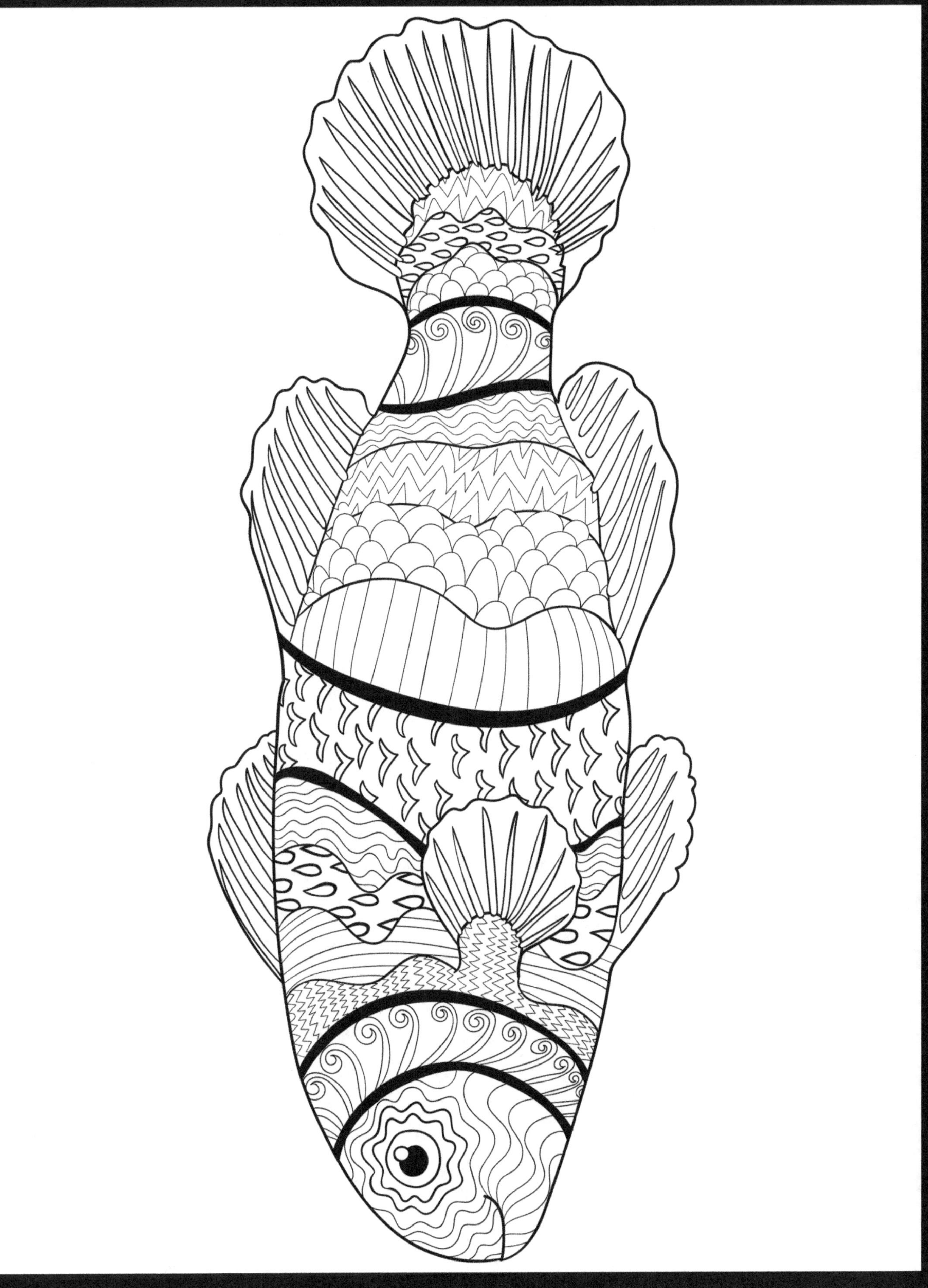

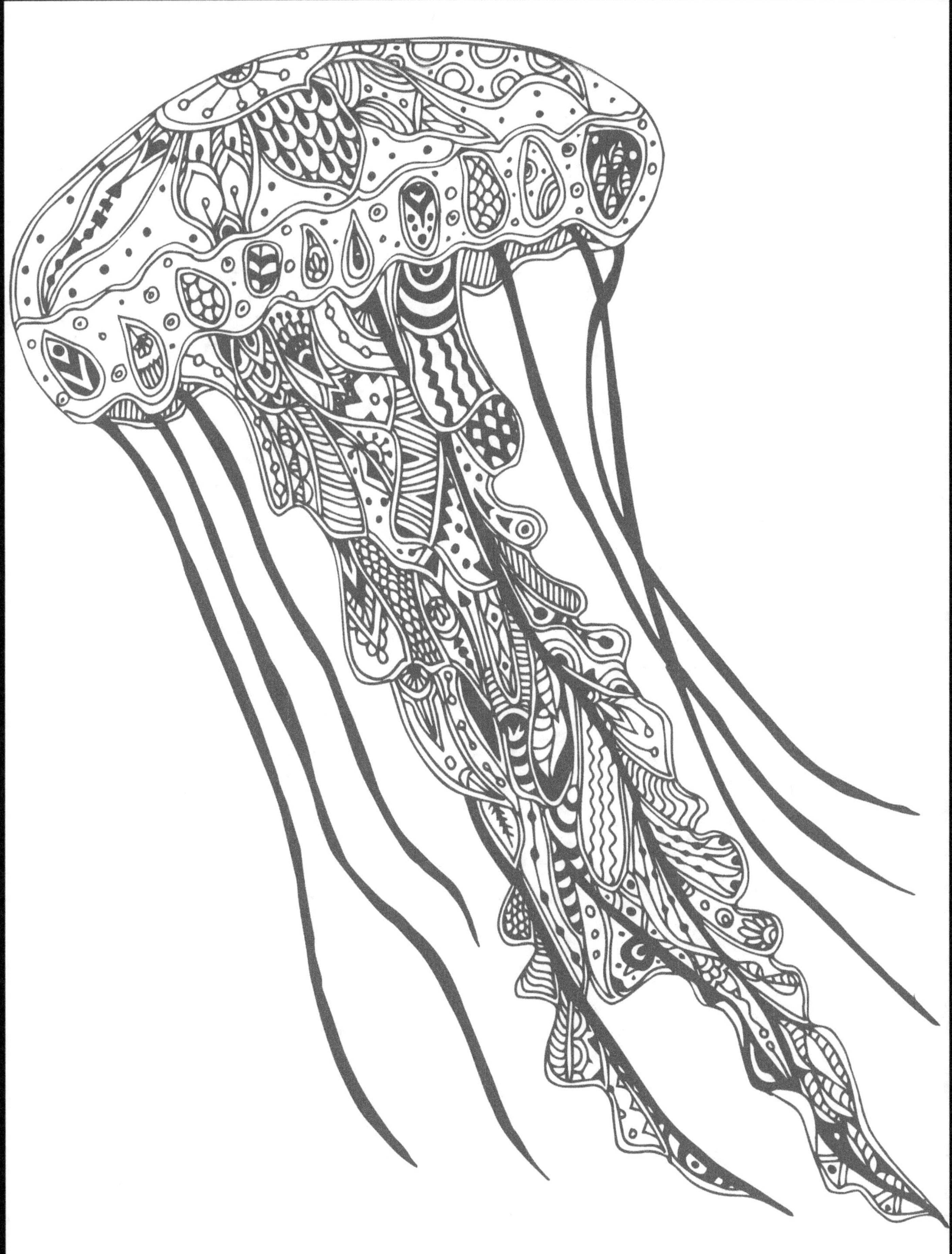